1

For all the kids that suffer due to parental conflict and divorce.

Ms. Ella Teaches Frankie to Speak-up!

Frankie grumbled to herself as she stomped into her new home. "Why did my parents have to get a divorce and wreck my life?!"

Frankie was not aware that Ms. Ella was listening. Frankie also did not realize that Ms. Ella was a tree. An ancient Talking Tree, hundreds and hundreds of years old. Talking Trees are very unique. They can communicate with some special children who understand Tree Talk. Frankie understood Tree Talk... she just didn't know it *yet*.

Friday finally came and after school, Frankie climbed up into Ms. Ella's big branches to have her snack and wait for her mom to return home from work. Frankie was happy it was Friday because it meant pizza and movie night with her mom.

Frankie was thinking about how much her life had changed since her parents' divorce, when suddenly, out of the blue, she heard a voice say, "Hello Frankie, I'm Ms. Ella". Frankie couldn't believe it! The *tree was talking* to her!

"Hi Ms. Ella" said Frankie, as if it was the most natural thing in the world to talk to a tree.

"Frankie, I can sense you are very unhappy. I want to help you if you would like me to."

"How can you help me Ms. Ella?" asked Frankie, curious about what Ms. Ella said.

"I'm going to teach you Tree Talk" said Ms. Ella matter-of-factly.

"What's Tree Talk?" asked Frankie, even more curious now.

"It's a natural ability that lies inside yourself Frankie, but you have to develop it if you want to feel happier."

"What natural ability?" asked Frankie. Instead of answering her as Frankie expected, Ms. Ella suddenly shook her branch, tossing Frankie to the ground where she landed on her bum and woke up.

"That was not very nice Ms. Ella, tossing me off your branch like that" said Frankie, brushing the dirt off her shorts. Ms. Ella didn't answer and when Frankie looked up, she saw a tree, just like every other tree.

Frankie wondered if she was dreaming, but didn't care because her mom was home and the pizza guy had arrived. Frankie ran to get the pizza and go inside for her favorite time of the whole week!

Frankie loved this new tradition she and her mom had started together. Her favorite thing was cuddling up with her mom, eating pizza and watching an exciting adventure movie together.

After the movie, Frankie brushed her teeth, hugged her mom and went to sleep. Soon she was back in Ms. Ella's branches. Frankie really wanted to know more about the natural ability she had to develop to become happier. "Wake up Ms. Ella!" Frankie whispered loudly.

"What? What? Am I dreaming again?" said Ms. Ella, yawning loudly.

"*Trees sleep?*" Frankie wondered in her head.

"Yes, of course we sleep. All living beings sleep" explained Ms. Ella.

"How did you know what I was thinking?" asked Frankie. "I didn't say anything out loud. I only thought it in my head. How did you know what I was thinking?"

"I know a lot of things" said Ms. Ella matter-of-factly.

"Oh yeah?" said Frankie, suddenly feeling upset. "Do you know why my parents got a divorce?" asked Frankie, a little more angrily than she meant to. She always got that yucky feeling in her body when she thought about her parents' divorce.

"Most parents get a divorce because they are not happy with each other anymore Frankie. Parents plan a life of happiness together and children, but then things happen and they stop listening to each other. Soon they can't solve their problems and can't live together peacefully and lovingly anymore, but they never stop being your parents and they *never* stop loving you. They may not be husband and wife anymore, but they are your mom and dad forever." said Ms. Ella in a gentle voice.

"I thought they hated each other and I thought I caused all the fighting between them" said Frankie sadly, as she remembered her parents fighting.

"Why would you think that, Frankie?"

"Because they were always fighting and many times I heard my name. I think they were fighting about me." Frankie got that upset feeling in her body again and felt like crying.

"I miss having two parents that love each other and I miss being normal like other kids. I miss goofing around with my dad whenever I want to. I miss my mom laughing... I miss so, so much" said Frankie, in a tearful voice.

"Your parents could not solve their problems Frankie, but I know for sure that they love you the same way they always have" said Ms. Ella. "And as for being normal, many families have problems. Some parents get divorced because that's the best way to solve their problems."

"What?" said Frankie, tilting her head a little to the left.

"It's true Frankie" said Ms. Ella. "Some families work out their problems by living together and some families work out their problems by living apart".

"Really?" said Frankie genuinely interested in what Ms. Ella was saying. "How can you stay together and stay apart and still be a family?"

"Families are connected in lots of ways Frankie. Sometimes it's better they live apart" explained Ms. Ella.

"Huh?" said Frankie, not completely understanding Ms. Ella.

"It's complicated Frankie. Let me explain it this way" said Ms. Ella. "When you first started school, you could read Dr. Seuss, but not Shakespeare. It takes time before you can read and understand Shakespeare. Does that make sense to you?"

"Yes, I think so" answered Frankie. "You're saying I have to be older to really understand complicated things like why parents get a divorce."

"Exactly!" exclaimed Ms. Ella. "Parents sometimes have different ideas about what's best for their children. Sometimes the differences are really big and parents argue. Parents sometimes completely forget to remember that their arguing is *really scary* for their children" explained Ms. Ella.

Frankie started getting that bad feeling in her body again just thinking about her parents not getting along. "I know!" exclaimed Frankie. "Every time I get upset, I can't think and I just don't know what to say. So, I hold my feelings inside and don't say anything at all." Frankie let out a deep sigh.

"Saying nothing at all is what brings on the bad feeling in your body Frankie" said Ms. Ella. "Most parents will help their children if they know what the problem is. But they can't help if you don't Speak Up about your problem."

"I would say something" answered Frankie, "but I'm scared to hurt their feelings, and sometimes they can get mad."

"Your parents are grown-ups Frankie. They would not want you to worry about them. In fact, I can tell you for sure that nothing makes a parent happier than seeing their child happy. Nothing at all!" said Ms. Ella in her wise and knowing voice that Frankie found comforting.

"When I get that yucky feeling in my body, I just don't know what to say" said Frankie. "I can't think straight."

"Nobody can think straight when they're very upset Frankie. The best thing to do when you're feeling upset is to take some slow deep breaths and give your brain more oxygen to think better with" said Ms. Ella as she stretched out her arms and took a slow deep tree breath. "Did you know, trees breathe in carbon dioxide and breathe out oxygen?" asked Ms. Ella.

 "I do know!" said Frankie, as she slowly exhaled her breath, imitating Ms. Ella. "And humans breathe in oxygen and breathe out carbon dioxide".

"Exactly, and do you know what that means Frankie?" asked Ms. Ella, slowly.

"It means we actually give each other what we need to stay alive," said Frankie slowly, as she paid attention to what she was saying.

"That's right Frankie, we cannot live without each other" said Ms. Ella, shimmering with delight at Frankie's First Tree Insight! "Well done Frankie! Now you're beginning to understand Tree Talk!" beamed Ms. Ella.

"I've never thought about it that way before" said Frankie thoughtfully, as she took more, slow, deep breaths.

Now that she was feeling calmer, Frankie could think more clearly and started to make a plan to tell her parents about her true thoughts and feelings. She was going to start with asking her mom if she could go to a special ball game with her dad on the weekend, even though it was her mom's weekend.

Just then, Ms. Ella decided it was the perfect moment to toss Frankie off of her branches and with a thud, Frankie landed on the ground, on her bum.

"You gotta stop doing that Ms. Ella" said Frankie as she brushed the dirt off her clothes and when she looked up at Ms. Ella, she saw a tree, just like every other tree.

The next night at dinner, Frankie was prepared. Frankie took a slow, deep breath and casually asked, "Mom, can I go to the ball game on Saturday with dad?"

"But it's our weekend together Frankie. I had plans for us" said her mom. Frankie was sure her mom sounded a little upset; she had that look on her face.

Frankie took another slow, deep breath and calmly said, "I know mom, but this Saturday is a very rare game. The Toronto Blue Jays are my favorite team and they're playing dad's favorite team, the Boston Red Sox's. It's a special game and I really, really, want to go! Can I please?" Frankie asked with as much confidence and calmness as she could muster.

Her mom looked carefully at Frankie and could see that going to the ball game with her dad was very important to her. She had that look on her face.

"You're right Frankie, it is a special game and I can make an exception this time. This is a very hard time for everyone, and especially you Frankie. Do you want to call your dad, or shall I?"

"I'll do it!" Frankie was out of her chair in no time, running to the phone.

"I'm sure going to the ball game with your dad will make him very happy too" her mother said out loud as Frankie was impatiently waiting for her dad to pick up the phone.

"Thanks for being such an awesome mom, mom" Frankie shouted back to her mom with a happy smile on her face. Frankie was elated. The ball game! Frankie spoke with her dad and of course, he was also excited to go. Frankie was very glad she listened to Ms. Ella and told her mom her true thoughts and feelings. She was proud she Spoke Up!

That night, Frankie was so excited, she could hardly sleep. Soon, she was in Ms. Ella's branches again.

"So, how did it go telling your parents what you truly think and feel?" asked Ms. Ella.

"It went great! Mom was awesome and me and my dad are going to the ball game on Saturday."

"Well done Frankie!" beamed Ms. Ella. "You seem happier already."

"I am. Thank you, Ms. Ella."

"For what Frankie?" asked Ms. Ella.

"For teaching me that I can do something about the bad feelings I get in my body. I can Speak Up and say what I truly think and feel in a calm and confident way."

Instead of saying 'you're welcome' like Frankie expected, Ms. Ella shook her branch and Frankie was tossed off, landing on her bum as usual.

"Why do you do that?" asked Frankie, slightly annoyed, as she shook the dirt off her pyjamas. She waited for Ms. Ella to answer, but she didn't. Frankie looked up and saw a tree, just like every other tree. She sighed and ran into the house to get ready for school.

Saturday finally came and Frankie was ready for her dad early and he came exactly on time, as usual. Her dad was so cool, even though the Red Sox were his team. Frankie had an amazing day cheering on her team, laughing at her dad cheering his team, eating popcorn, being silly and just having fun. After an exciting game, the Red Sox won.

Frankie was happy and they both celebrated together. It was her tradition with her dad to get an ice cream cone for the drive back, listen to loud music and sing even louder all the way home. She loved this time with her dad.

At the end of the day, Frankie collapsed into her bed, happy and exhausted after a day filled with laughter and happiness. She lay in bed thinking how amazing it was that her life changed so easily and so quickly. Just by learning how to stay calm and Speaking Up Frankie was able to change the way she felt in her body. She wasn't feeling sad and angry any more.

Before she fell asleep, Frankie noticed that her body was quiet like a tree. She realized she was feeling calm in her body, the way she used to feel before her parents started arguing, and before their divorce. She had almost forgotten that calm quiet feeling in her body. Frankie fell asleep thinking that she needed to learn more things from Ms. Ella. She planned to talk again with her, and soon, Frankie found herself in Ms. Ella's branches, as usual.

Frankie started telling Ms. Ella about her amazing day with her dad, but Ms. Ella abruptly shook her branch and Frankie fell out of the tree, but this time, Frankie was ready for Ms. Ella's toss. This time, Frankie quickly focused her attention and landed gracefully on her feet, like there was no gravity.

"Ahhh..... Hahahahaha!" Ms. Ella laughed out loud. "I was wondering when you'd figure that out" she chuckled, glad that Frankie finally realized she did not have to fall on her bum every time a branch shook.

"Until the next time Tree Talker!!" said Ms. Ella with a happy grin. "Thanks you so much" said Frankie as she gave Ms. Ella a big tree hug and said "Until the next time Ms. Ella". Frankie walked away happily and when she looked up, she saw a tree just like every other tree.

Dawn DeCunha is a Psychologist who has worked with children and their families for most of her career. While she does a lot of professional writing, this is her first children's book. She continues to practice in the Toronto area and lives with her two children and gentle Komondor, Marley.

Claudia Varjotie is a Brazilian illustrator who graduated with a degree in Architecture and Urban Design. After 10 years of practice in her profession, she moved to Finland where she had more time to concentrate on her art and discover her love for Children's Book Illustrations. She moved back to Brazil and lives with her three children Iago, Lars and Anna Lis and rescued dog Luna.

www.ingramcontent.com/pod-product-compliance
Lightning Source LLC
Chambersburg PA
CBHW041806040426
42448CB00005B/290